AF866832

The Quiet Age

The Quiet Age

CREATING A CALM LIFE IN A CHAOTIC WORLD

CORY ALLEN

Andrews McMeel
PUBLISHING®

to Meredith

CONTENTS

01 RESET

In a world that's addicted to urgency,

moving slowly is an act of rebellion.

Say goodbye to urgency culture. You don't have to reply to that message now. Your email can wait. You don't have to live with anxiety because of the expectations of others. Let yourself be human instead of forcing yourself to be a machine. Your heart, nervous system, and adrenal glands will thank you.

UNDERRATED LIFE SKILLS:

Letting people be wrong about you.

Knowing when to walk away.

Leaving behind what no longer aligns.

Enjoying where you are without rushing.

Being okay with not having all the answers.

Choosing to rest and not force progress.

You are allowed to disconnect

and disappear for a while.

The world will go on without you.

But you will come back to yourself.

GENTLE REMINDER:

Not everything needs healing.

Some things just need leaving.

If burning out were the answer, it would have worked already. We know this is true. Yet the conditioned connection between self-worth and progress forces us into survival mode.

Here, we feel an anxious need to overspend our energy, grind ourselves down, and power ahead under the illusion that being exhausted proves that we have earned our value.

When you notice you're drained of energy but feel pressured to keep going, remember that *actual* progress follows rest, not exhaustion.

CLARITY IS KNOWING:

Your worth is remembered,

not earned.

Some conversations are invitations to exhaustion.

Decline softly.

Your nervous system can get so used
to anxiety that ease feels unnatural.

But the more you choose to slow down,
let your body soften and your mind quiet,
the more you'll see that you're not meant
to live in constant tension.

You're meant for soft, spacious peace.

You're meant to feel at home in yourself.

Breathe deeply. Relax your muscles.

Come home.

You're taught to chase what

looks good from the outside.

Now—

Try seeking what feels good

on the inside.

Learning to step back from urgency culture isn't about ghosting the world and ignoring your responsibilities. It's about learning how to take back part of your life so you can prioritize your happiness and stop feeling so overwhelmed and undernourished.

Some things deserve your
absence, not your energy.

Peace begins with reconnection.

Slow down. Listen within. Notice your
thoughts, emotions, and impulses.

Then soften. Let go of impulses as they arise,
dissolve old patterns, and release the idea that
you always have to be doing something.

Reset the tempo of your being to one
that feels natural, instead of rushed.

Your nervous system will regulate as you
start moving at a slower pace.

Then a space will open inside of you.

In that space, you can hear your intuition,
think clearly, and start guiding your life from
a place of purpose instead of pressure.

REMINDER:

Taking a break is how you
keep from breaking.

You might think that being busy makes you important. That rushing means you're doing something meaningful. That a packed social life means you're truly connecting.

You might think that constant motion means you're getting somewhere. But really, it just pulls you further from yourself.

When you slow down, you begin to feel the pain you've been trying to outrun. Your awareness steadies. Your mind clears. Healing begins.

Each day, you start to listen to what you feel, honor what you need, and release the habits that hurt you.

The heaviness lifts, and in its place grows the most beautiful peace.

Healing begins when we stop
mistaking our survival patterns
for our personality.

Listen within yourself. Feel the heaviness you're carrying, see the patterns you're repeating, and hear the echoes of pain that live in you.

Be patient, gentle, and honest. Notice when you react out of fear, rush for no reason, and slide into survival mode. Don't feel guilty when it happens. You've been living this way for a long time.

But no more.

Break old habits by choosing new behaviors in the present moment.

Spend less time with people who drain you and more with people who make you feel aligned.

Listen to what you need in each moment, and give yourself the respect you deserve by honoring it.

Take up space. You have the right to exist in your peace, exhale, and *be here as you are.*

Let go of the heaviness. Rest in the now.

The tension you carry will ripple
into how you see everything
until you slow down and
gently start letting go.

Give yourself rest.

Give yourself love.

Give yourself time.

Give yourself space.

Give yourself patience.

Give yourself gentleness.

Don't worry what other people think.

You're not doing it for them.

You're doing it for you.

The world will not slow down for you.

The world will keep taking from you.

The world will trick you into believing
that anxiety and tension are best for you.

So you must slow down for yourself.

You must choose to give yourself the
nurturing and validation you were
hoping to get from the world.

The first time you let a message
sit unread without guilt, you'll
feel a freedom you didn't know
you were missing.

One of the most powerful
things you can do is choose
not to engage.

You don't have to be overwhelmed
to slow down. You just have to be ready
to feel the simple depth of your life, instead
of the tense drama of your mental story.

REMEMBER:

Here is the only place you need to be.

The story in your mind isn't reality.

Don't take a bad day personally.

Precision is stronger than force.

Stopping for the day is okay.

Clarity comes through calm.

Tension is only temporary.

Peace lives in deep breath.

When you feel anxiety, imagine what you would see if you watched a video recording of yourself in that moment.

Inside, your nerves are electric, your heart races, and your mind swims with fearful possibilities.

But the video would show the truth.

You're just a person sitting safely in a room.

The fear in your mind is a projection, not reality.

Grounding yourself in the truth of the present moment will soften your reactions and bring healing clarity to your fearful mental stories.

Peace begins there.

Sometimes you have to be honest with yourself about how others make you feel. If you're tense, down, or empty after being with someone, it could mean that you don't align with them for now.

Or for good.

When you feel this, ask yourself:

If I met this person as they are today instead of as they were when I first met them, would I still want to spend time with them?

If the answer is no, it could mean that you need to give that relationship space.

Let them relearn you. Relearn them. Then decide whether you want to reintroduce the current version of them into the life you're living now.

Clarity begins when you stop
letting your past speak for you
and start listening to how you
actually feel in the present.

When you stop rushing, the world around you slows down too.

Conversations deepen. Tasks lose their urgency. Senses sharpen. Clarity awakens. Silence begins to feel calming rather than overwhelming.

By moving at your own peaceful tempo, you give your nervous system a signal of safety. This lets you calm down on an animal level. No more looking for threats in the environment. No more panic.

Moving like this opens a portal to a new way of being. It reveals the ease, wonder, and joy that have spent so much time behind an illusion of pressure.

It's time you stopped meeting
the standards of others and started
prioritizing your own.

Forget about what works for everyone else.

They aren't you.

Find what brings you calm, joy, and safety.

Then do it often.

It can be a practice, ritual, therapy, or pastime. It can be big, small, cheap, expensive, cool, or out of style. It doesn't matter *what* it is.

It matters what it *does*.

Find the special thing, just for you, that gives you life, makes you feel like the most authentic version of yourself, and pulls you right into the present moment.

Then cherish it.

Feeling fidgety when you're
trying to slow down is a sign
you're almost there.

Keep going.

That feeling will melt away.

Your body and mind are just
relearning what it means
to be at ease.

Being present not only grounds you
but also shares your sturdy calm
with everyone around you.

It's hard to see the positive changes in your life at first. That's because peace doesn't flick on like a light switch. It fades in.

Watch your mind, slow your reactions, and let go when you feel tension trying to take over. Doing this takes you off autopilot and gives you the chance in each moment to rewrite who you are.

Since you're working against years of conditioning, it will take some patience. But don't stop when you start doubting yourself.

One day, you'll notice more room in the present. You'll find yourself choosing your words as you speak, releasing triggers before they go off, and feeling calm in moments when you used to feel tension.

Then it will hit you that the effort you're putting in has already begun changing everything.

Decide that harmony is nonnegotiable.

Stop waiting for permission, and softly say,

This is what matters in my life from here on.

Not out of anger but toward alignment.

Not with force but with steadiness.

Not out of fear but toward self-trust.

Not with reactivity but with resolve.

You're done suffering from anxiety, drama,

and the wounded vulnerability of the past.

You're done rushing on behalf of people who

don't give you time or energy in return.

You choose to let go and find your peace.

You choose to be firm and take up space.

You choose to follow what feels right.

You choose to soften and open up again.

It's a new chapter.

The real flex is knowing when
to walk away. Not because you're
bitter but because you're done
accepting less than you deserve.

A SIMPLE WAY TO IMPROVE YOUR LIFE:

Pause and feel what's true for you in the present, instead of being controlled by your past.

Clear inner guidance comes from
knowing the difference between
your ego and your heart.

Your ego shouts.

Your heart whispers.

Peace begins when you realize
everyone sees the world through
a different lens and it's not your
job to polish theirs.

Some people might not understand
why you need more space.

They may take it personally when you
don't respond to texts or emails quickly.

Let them know you're not connecting
to your digital life as often because you
need less noise right now.

Clearly communicating that your slower
responses aren't personal builds healthy,
relaxed rhythms of connection.

Spending time alone is healing
because your nervous system can
drop its defenses and safely begin
to soften, rest, and reset to its
natural state of calm.

It can feel uneasy to bring more quiet into your life. Noise felt normal. So the stress and constant stimulation felt natural.

The noise was numbing your sensitivity.

When the noise stops, your feelings, thoughts, and body signals become clear. This can feel intense to your ego and might tempt you to go back to numbing yourself with noise.

That discomfort eases quickly.

Your nervous system will start to regulate. You'll feel lighter, and life will glow in a way that it hasn't for a long time.

You'll feel calm yet full of vibrance.

You'll shine like the sun, radiating stillness.

TO SEE CLEARLY:

Pause.

Take a breath.

Let go of the old story.

Allow the present to speak.

Calm is wisdom.

It helps you notice reactive patterns and
choose actions that are aligned with today.

It helps you see reality clearly and release old
anxieties that have been holding you back.

It helps you feel your flow, so you can stop
doubting yourself and move forward.

It helps you monitor your mind and let go
of thoughts that aren't helpful.

It helps you hear your intuition and choose
what feels right again and again.

Feeling overwhelmed but choosing not to take it out on others is a sign that your compassion and awareness have grown into wisdom.

Stillness focuses the blur of reality.

Mindful clarity helps you see the subtle kindness, love, and tenderness of others. It also shows you the selfishness, contradictions, and hidden motives that some people carry.

It's important to remember that everyone has massive gaps in their awareness. They may not be conscious of their actions, whether kind or cold. Often, they're simply running scripts that were activated in childhood and don't know any other way to be.

As you begin to see a deeper layer of reality, don't weigh yourself down with judgment. Accept people as they are. Become a grounded source of awareness, kindness, and calm.

Simply lead by example as a beacon of insight, integrity, and harmony.

You can move at your own speed
and let the world bend around you,
or you can move at the world's pace
and be bent by the world.

GENTLE REMINDER:

There are rarely any moments

when you actually need to rush.

Are you holding tension, breathing shallow, and hurrying from one thing to the next because you need to or because it's what you're used to?

Being in survival mode is painful because we panic through life, scanning for threats, always reacting in a defensive, protective, or anxious way. We fear what's next instead of feeling excitement. We put up walls instead of opening ourselves to feeling known on the deepest level.

It's not our fault that we live in survival mode. Something happened, likely in our youth, that created a core wound. That wound shaped a deep layer of our personality, skill set, and view of reality. Since then, we fought our way forward, creating the safest life possible, telling ourselves the cost of numbness was worth the stability.

We don't have to define ourselves by our core wounds. It is possible to heal, repattern, and reemerge into a new life of trust and love.

Awareness is everything. Watch your mind, reactions, and emotions. When survival habits ping, take a breath, label them for what they are, and choose a new behavior in the present.

Step by step, moment to moment, you can gently reshape your inner habits, open your heart, feel safe again, and start living *your life* instead of the life your wounds made you believe was necessary.

02 SLOW

UNDERRATED LIFE SKILLS:

Pausing to decide if it's worth your energy.

Not confusing moving fast with moving forward.

Knowing that clarity comes after rest, not effort.

Saying no without giving a long explanation.

Moving on without needing closure.

Peace doesn't come from controlling everything. It comes from learning what's worth your energy and what isn't.

A SIMPLE WAY TO IMPROVE YOUR LIFE:

Be clear on who gets your time, who gets your energy, and who gets nothing.

You are not behind.

There is no timeline.

You haven't lost your way.

You are carving a new path.

You are not moving too slowly.

You are living at the speed of peace.

Question your first reaction. Get curious about why you want to control things. Ask what wound was touched when you feel yourself put up a wall.

See yourself clearly.

Look inward, not to judge but to understand.

Self-awareness is gentle but powerful. It's how you see what's shaping your mind. Once you notice your behaviors in real time, you can choose to respond to them in a way that serves you better.

Bring compassion to what you see about yourself. Only then will your ego, heart, and history release the old patterns and make room for a liberated version of you to come through.

Peace comes when you accept reality.

That doesn't mean you give up. It means you let yourself see things as they really are.

It means you no longer delude yourself into taking less than you deserve. You stop ignoring loud signals and red flags. You don't talk yourself out of seeing the truth so you can avoid conflict or temporary discomfort.

You realize that numbness is a silent form of pain. And you're tired of living that way. So you start accepting reality and responding accordingly.

You speak up. You stop shrinking. You let people who don't treat you well go their own way.

You take action *in flow with truth* instead of against it. By doing so, your actions connect with what's real—instead of with a false mental story—and true change begins to unfold.

Clarity arrives when
the mind stops clinging
to the story it's creating.

Slowing down is the superpower
that lets you listen deeply, speak
clearly, choose wisely, and love fully.

Being present is like opening a window to a deeper layer of truth. That's why so many people disassociate to avoid it.

Use your courage to slow down and be honest with yourself. See where you need nourishment, the tricks you're using to keep yourself detached, and the *reason* you seek the forms of numbness that you do.

Then give yourself what you need.

Give yourself love, gentleness, patience, trust, and calmness. Look deeply at what's causing your pain and heal it with the soft, accepting presence of your heart.

Letting go gets easier when
you realize the things you're
holding on to only have meaning
because you gave it to them.

Urgency is rarely real, but your nervous
system often forgets that's true.

When you're tense, lost in a mental story,
and stuck on autopilot, remember to let
yourself breathe before you react.

You'll see that the stress was just a narrative
in your mind that felt real.

You'll see that most things can wait.

You don't need more time.

You need to stop spending time

on things that don't matter.

Peace is more valuable than perception.

People won't always understand why you need to disappear, do you, and recharge for a while.

That's fine, because you aren't doing it for them.

You're doing it for you.

UNDERRATED LIFE SKILL:

Choosing calm when

others expect a reaction.

Giving yourself space from the noise in life won't heal where you're hurting. But it *will* quiet the static in your mind so you can see your pains clearly.

Knowing what habits are keeping you stuck and which pains need healing is the first step to changing your entire way of being.

Seeing yourself clearly is what gives you the capacity to let go, embrace truths, and make meaningful choices that create real change.

Give your mind quiet so you can hear.

Then look honestly at the world within you.

During the day, start to notice your reactive patterns, thinking habits, and emotional armor.

Gently shift them as they rise by choosing actions that align with who you are today rather than who you were in the past.

Doing this work takes patience.

It's repetitive. It's messy. It's full of learning.

But it's the only way to retrain the ingrained patterns that are weighing you down and move toward a life of harmony.

There was a time when

silence felt uncomfortable.

Now it feels like home.

Slowing down isn't about detaching from life. It's about giving yourself the space to look deeply at reality so you can consciously live the life you want, instead of the one dealt to you by the randomness of the universe.

Conscious untangling is what
helps you develop mental clarity.

It's refusing to replay the same
emotional and intellectual loops.

It's listening to what you're feeling
in the moment and honoring it.

It's noticing the internal patterns
that are limiting your happiness.

It's trusting your intuition and
making choices that feel right.

Slow down,

see your habits,

hear your intuition,

honor what you feel,

guide yourself clearly,

give yourself peace.

You won't realize how tense you are
until you finally let yourself slow down.

Your shoulders will drop, and your
breath will deepen.

Your mind will clear of static, and your
emotions will calm.

Your feet will touch the ground, and you'll
feel the ground touching you back.

You'll see that everything you are seeking
is already waiting for you in the present.

Your desire to live in a rush will fade.

You'll let go of the noise and refocus on
presence, kindness, and the calm of now.

We feel we have to say yes to everything

because we're taught to always take on more.

Try pausing before you answer.

Ask yourself: *Do I actually want this?*

We normalize stress, anxiety, and exhaustion
because we are designed to adapt.

We slowly accept suffering and numbness
until it's all we can see.

We mislabel that pain as "what life is" and
forget that other ways of living are possible.

We can't see how much tension we live with
until we soften.

We can't see how much we are carrying
until we slow down.

We can't feel how much we are grasping
until we finally let go.

You're under no obligation
to keep being who you were
yesterday just because it's what
others are comfortable with.

Who you are is only an idea. An expression of self, shaped by memory, experience, and environment.

None of it is permanent. Your needs evolve, your preferences shift, and your values mature. But you stay attached to the idea of who you are because it's what you are used to.

Yet the truth is that you are free.

You're allowed to release the roles you were praised for. You can grow past the persona that you built to feel safe. You don't owe anyone, or yourself, the performance of an outdated version of who you are.

The self isn't a prison. It is a space for you to keep clearing, refining, and reshaping as your awareness deepens.

This is why quiet matters. Because the quieter you become, the more clearly you can see yourself and the more easily you can step out of past patterns and into alignment.

Who you are isn't an unchangeable truth.

It's a story you can rewrite whenever your heart feels you're ready.

When you first slow down,

you might not know how to

be alone with your thoughts.

You'll find that you want to

fill the gaps with noise.

Release into the stillness.

The discomfort will melt.

You'll find something beautiful.

Yourself.

Next time you get frustrated that
someone isn't responding to your
message fast enough, remember how
peaceful it feels when you're living
in the freedom of the present,
removed from digital life.

Focus less on how fast you respond
and more on the care you put into
your words when you do.

Today, silence your phone
and leave it in another room.

Sit with your coffee or tea in the calm
stillness of quiet, and watch the light
in the room move across the floor.

Nothing will happen. And yet you'll
feel like more has happened than you
can remember in a long time.

PEACE LOOKS LIKE:

Past understood.

Present honored.

Future welcomed.

Notice that when you're rushing, anxious, and on autopilot, it's usually in response to someone or something outside of yourself.

You feel that tension because your natural speed is slower than what urgency culture demands.

Give yourself the space to live at your own tempo.

Take plenty of time to exist in a restful state without committing to too much. Plan ahead so you don't feel the panic of rushing.

Rest in the calm clarity of your own speed.

Breathe deeply. Relax your muscles.

Let your mind cool off, wander, and rewire.

This spaciousness is where you can connect with a deep part of your human nature. One of peace, presence, and easeful clarity.

It's hard to see yourself when you stay too busy. Constant distraction numbs the sensitivity you need to feel what's happening inside of you.

Stillness creates space for honest insight. It shows you what you need and what you're ignoring.

You can ignore an inner truth for years. But when you slow down and calm your body, your inner world can calm too. And when your inner world is calm, you can start to see.

Slowness creates self-intimacy that lets you gently embrace your inner truths, integrate them, and finally give them the respect they deserve.

Your mind is like a lake.

Busy thoughts create ripples in the water.
Light dances off the waves, and while
it's pretty, it's only surface level.

A calm mind with less stimulation
has fewer agitated thoughts. Without
ripples, the water is smooth and clear.

In a still lake, you can see your reflection.
You can also look through the surface of
the water and see into the depths below.

When your mind is calm, you can see clearly
while still being aware of your own reflection.

Until you understand your own
patterns, perceptions, and pains,
you'll keep mistaking them
for someone else's.

The more deeply you look into yourself,

the more deeply you can see into others.

Gently exploring deeper levels of your mind offers invaluable insight not only into yourself but into all human beings.

Once you know the depths of your own joy, hope, love, fear, anger, and pain, you learn that those feelings don't exist only in you.

They exist in everyone.

This humble wisdom gives you more compassion, patience, and understanding for everyone you meet because you see yourself in them.

It reminds you that beneath the surface, most people just want to feel loved, safe, and known.

Knowledge of our shared human experience makes what truly matters clear: kindness, connection, empathy, and care.

A SIMPLE WAY TO IMPROVE YOUR LIFE:

Notice how your nervous system responds to people's energy, not just the words they say.

You will have ups and downs.
Your mood will sharpen and soften.
Your mind will expand and contract.
Your heart will cool and warm.

No matter what happens in the present,
as long as your intentions are harmony,
compassion, and balance, you will always
find your way back to a peaceful life.

Always.

SLOWING DOWN IS NOT:

Being irresponsible, ignoring people, isolating yourself, and giving up on goals.

SLOWING DOWN IS:

Responding with intention instead of reacting with tension, giving yourself the space to feel what you need, and living at a tempo that feels natural.

Slowing down helps you notice
when you're no longer chasing
the experience but the illusion
of control behind it.

Our ego tries to control life so we can believe that we are safe. But life isn't controllable. So the mind grows a habit of grasping at control anywhere it can.

We enter a kind of psychological survival mode. The ego gets fixated on gaining anything that feels like it might protect us from the uncertainty of life. Often, that is more power, status, and money.

This is why working all the time, competing with everyone, feeling guilty for resting, and tying our worth to how much we achieve becomes so easily normalized.

At some point, we forgot that all we were ever trying to do was feel safe, and we ended up becoming the very threat we wanted to protect ourselves from.

Desire can feel exciting and meaningful at first. But after a while, we notice that the high of wanting is usually followed by a low mood. After living this cycle enough times, we start looking for a way out.

When the mind realizes it's stuck in a loop of craving and disappointment, the pull of desire begins to fade.

We start to see reality more clearly.

We get free.

When we resist chasing the next thing, working constantly, scrolling endlessly, and denying ourselves rest, rushing starts to feel unnecessary.

So we slow down, take care of ourselves, and deeply enjoy the small, meaningful moments in life.

We remember that desire promises happiness in the future, but awareness finds peace in the present.

When your mind draws you
back into a habit of rushing,
reactivity, and relentlessness,
let it be a reminder of why you
slowed down in the first place.

It's okay to breathe.

It's okay to want less.

It's okay to be alone.

It's okay to need quiet.

It's okay to talk less.

It's okay to just be.

Each time you soften your body

and mind, return to the truth:

You are not fixed. You're changing.

You are awareness, forever growing.

You are love, gently finding its way.

Quiet is clarity, the path to peace.

Letting go isn't about not caring,
giving up, or becoming passive.

It's about recognizing the hollowness
of passing tensions in life and refusing
to let them influence your emotions,
thoughts, or inner harmony.

Peace is already here.

You just have to stop reacting

to the world around you

long enough to see it.

We cling to the known and resist change
because it seems safe. But the reality is that
everything is always changing on its own.

Clinging creates conflict because as we stay
attached to the idea that makes us feel safe,
it has changed in a way we don't want to see.

Much of our suffering is tied to the fact that
we'd rather cling to the harmful known
than travel an unfamiliar path.

Shift your mindset. Welcome the unknown.
It will show you the possibilities in everything
and open paths around every turn.

Meeting the present with a trust that change is happening *for you,* not *to you,* is how you bend reality in your favor and expand your universe.

A life focused on gentleness, harmony,
and peace may seem so spacious at first
that you feel lost.

Give it time.

A new way of seeing will fade in, and
you'll see that space isn't nothingness.

It's freedom.

03 DISCOVER

If it drains you every time,

your nervous system is telling

you to move on.

THE MIND WILL MAKE YOU:

Chase what you think completes you.

Hold tightly to what you think defines you.

Look for answers that promise to fix everything.

Compare your life to the illusions of others.

Crave what pulls you away from the present.

Go ahead.

Look for as long as you need to see that peace
isn't out there in any of those things.

It was always waiting quietly within you.

When you see that, you can stop searching
for approval, clarity, and direction.

You can let go of what you were chasing, come
home to yourself, and finally feel the peace
you were searching for.

You don't improve your life
by doing more. You improve it by
doing less of what doesn't matter.

Peace isn't something you find.
It's something you create. Every choice
you make to let go, slow down, soften
your ego, release bad habits, and bring
compassion forward is what builds it.

Don't worry about

being liked by everyone.

Half of them don't even

like themselves.

GENTLE REMINDER:

Your nervous system
is a better compass than
other people's opinions.

It's okay not to know where you're going.
Just don't keep moving in directions you know
aren't for you. When you stop choosing what
isn't right, life will guide you to what is.

People in your life might not understand your change at first.

When you start speaking gently, moving more slowly, and offering more truth, it can feel confusing to people who already think of you in a certain way.

They may try hard to pull you into old habits that are familiar to them.

Don't take it personally. Their ego is looking for a way to feel steady after your change.

Treat the moment gently. Stay aligned in who you are becoming. And remember why you decided to start changing in the first place.

A SIMPLE WAY TO IMPROVE YOUR LIFE:

Stop trying to be understood by people who don't understand themselves.

Your nervous system always knows
who the real ones are. Listen closely.

Forget about what other people think

or who culture says you should be.

Listen within.

Become a student of your own heart and mind.

See your inner life shift as you keep focusing on

compassion, calmness, and mental clarity.

Notice how today you're more conscious

than you were three months ago.

Let that growth inspire you to keep going.

And remember how far you've come

the next time you doubt yourself.

People are attracted to energy.

Putting out the vibration of peace, clarity, and good values means those who find you will be doing the same.

Positive energy is an invitation that brings the right people into your life.

How could anyone else
know what's right for you
when they aren't you?

Walling off our emotions is how we try to create a sense of safety and control.

But as we spend more time in the quiet, we hear ourselves more deeply and start to realize we aren't safe behind our wall.

We've created a world of isolation, numbness, and distance.

We may learn how to let go of thoughts and emotions, but eventually we realize the real challenge is letting go of the space we've created between ourselves and the world.

Slowly, we can begin to share more honestly and stop hiding behind the intellect.

As we do so, the wall comes down, and we find what was missing that made us feel so alone.

Real connection.

Core wounds from the past influence your emotions in the present. Emotional reactions are usually less about what is happening now and more about what happened back then.

Knowing this lets you see these moments with fresh clarity, giving you the opportunity to unhook from your old wounds by tending to the moment in a new way.

Past experiences condition the way you see reality and yourself. Stillness gives you the inner clarity to see not only who you were but who you are today and who you can become in the future.

Knowing that your perception is influenced by the past gives you the power to see your doubts, limiting beliefs, and negative self-image as the false thoughts they are.

Label these thoughts as false when they come to mind. Throw them out. Then move forward with self-belief that's grounded in who you are today, not who you were.

Spending time with less input and a slower tempo of being gives you the chance to understand new things about yourself.

Don't force them.

Allow self-knowledge to appear in its own time. It's an organic process. When insights arise, receive them, turn them into action, and move forward with a fresh perspective.

Low moods lie to you about your worth.

After periods of letting go, you may feel a subtle sense of loss. This is the feeling of saying goodbye to an old self-image that's no longer a part of you.

For a time, that identity may have served you well, but you've grown past it, and it is no longer what you need to thrive. Let the old you go, and look ahead to the expanded path that awaits you.

The first time you choose to rest without letting
yourself feel guilty, you might feel like
you are breaking a rule.

Like your value as a human dropped because
you are no longer being productive.

But the more you choose to rest without worry,
the more you'll realize that rest was never the enemy.

It is the missing piece that will help you become
who you have been wanting to be all along.

If you never slow down,

how will you ever be able

to tell if you're going in

the right direction?

Wisdom is seeing reality clearly. Each moment is perceived through the filter of your emotional history, defenses, desires, and insecurities.

Knowing this lets you perceive the moment for what it is, compare it to the story in your mind, then consider what's actually happening from multiple perspectives.

Noting your perception, then thinking beyond your personal bias, is how you get closer to truth, peace, and a life of harmony.

Mindfulness is being aware of your actions,
thoughts, impulses, and emotional reactions
in the present moment.

Mindful living is monitoring those things
and intentionally guiding them toward
compassion, kindness, and clarity.

Cultivating quiet in your life creates a new kind of internal awareness.

The relationship with your mind expands, and you see your mental narratives as stories, rather than being caught within their drama.

Observing your thoughts as they gently flow across the stage of your mind gives you the space to see arising thoughts, reactions, and impulses as suggestions rather than instructions.

Viewing your inner landscape in such a way makes it easier to let go of unhelpful thoughts, release reactions, and disrupt mental noise.

Most important, it exposes the truth that you are not your thoughts. You are the thoughts you turn into action.

Your thoughts aren't the problem.

Your belief in them is.

Our minds are layered in memory. Everything that came before this moment has left an impression upon our consciousness.

Defensiveness, insecurity, fear, prejudice, and bias trigger easily in the present, like traps snapping shut. These traps are there to protect us from reliving the suffering that set them in the first place.

Mindful living slows our reactions and helps us experience the present moment for what it is, rather than through the filter of memory.

Practicing mindfulness rewrites our mental patterns, allowing us to exit survival mode, feel safe, and experience living in a world of peaceful curiosity instead of fearful contraction.

Notice how your mind rushes ahead,

pulling you into a future that doesn't exist.

Come back.

Right here in this moment is where

your life is happening.

A quiet life is not an empty life.

It is a life of depth, meaning,

and the things that truly matter.

Self-awareness is clarity. But it's hard
to develop if the mind is overwhelmed
with constant input.

Turn down the noise of digital life, and
give yourself the space to live more slowly.
Your natural flow will realign, and your
mind will clear on its own.

Once you see how old patterns
try to control you in the present,
reshaping them becomes possible.

The more stillness you invite into your life, the more clearly you can hear your deeper self. Beneath the mental noise, there is a voice that knows how to support you. Listen closely to it and you'll never be without a teacher.

UNDERRATED LIFE SKILLS:

Listening to what feels right.

Knowing what recharges you.

Letting go of expectations.

Choosing instead of reacting.

Waiting for what takes time.

Awareness shows us
that negativity fades
when you stop giving
it attention.

Remove the words "I," "me," and "my" from your thinking and you'll see reality for what it is instead of what you're forcing it to be.

The ego forces itself into every experience,
which is why even small frictions cause reactions.

Watching for this habit shows you that not only
is most tension meaningless, but it likely has
nothing to do with you in the first place.

Life is just *happening*, not happening *to you.*

Remember this when drama, conflict,
or noise creates tension inside you.

The mind quickly builds a story about "me"
and "my problem," and this story fuels
your emotions.

But life is unfolding on its own. Most things
aren't personal. Just events moving through
time, here in one moment and gone the next.

Let go of the story and mental drama.

Return your attention to the calm life
flowing in front of you.

No matter what's happening
in the world, in your home, or in your
body, your heart and mind will always
be safe places of refuge and freedom.

The world will keep trying to fill you up
with opinions, expectations, and tension.

Real peace comes when you refuse those
things and exist in your own way, in your
own time, moving in peaceful harmony.

It's not about always being perfectly mindful.

It's about building a life that thrives on compassion, kindness, calm, self-awareness, and good intentions.

That way, even when you're wrong, you're right.

SIGNS YOU ARE LIVING MINDFULLY:

You inhale before you respond.

You choose presence over distraction.

You pause and see your thoughts clearly.

You can sit in stillness without restlessness.

You don't need to rush what unfolds naturally.

You listen to understand instead of to respond.

You invite change without grasping at the past.

You move from intention instead of impulse.

You feel contentment in ordinary moments.

Inhaling before you respond gives your nervous system a chance to reset.

That single breath interrupts your emotional reaction and creates space for awareness.

With a pause, you can slow your mind, regulate your tone, and respond in a thoughtful, compassionate way.

Choosing presence over distraction means consciously breaking the habit of scrolling on your phone, always having stimulation, and feeling the need to oversocialize.

When you're constantly feeding distractions into your mind, there's no space for you to reflect and connect with your deeper self.

Through cultivating more stillness and calm in your life, you'll not only think more clearly but also be a clearer version of yourself.

Most suffering comes from the story in your mind, not the reality in front of you. Pausing to see your thoughts clearly helps you separate your mental story and what's actually happening. Assumptions, projections, and false narratives fall away, giving you a clearer view of life and relief from the pain caused by the mind.

Constant restlessness is a sign that your nervous system is stuck in a reactive loop. Take time to sit, breathe calmly, and relax the muscles in your body as you exhale.

Your nervous system will rewire, the restlessness will dissolve, and you'll be able to rest deeply within yourself.

Your thoughts will calm, your mind will focus, and your awareness will clear. This is a step toward authentic inner peace.

Craving instant gratification makes us rush through things that actually need time. Not everything is meant to be quick or disposable.

The things that grow slowly grow deeply, last longer, and become more meaningful.

When you stop forcing and allow things to unfold, you build a life rooted in alignment instead of impatient fear.

Human life is about resonance.

We are always searching for people who see the world the way we do, because when we find them, we feel less alone.

Resonance doesn't just come from talking. It comes from listening, dropping judgment, holding back assumptions, and being present enough to recognize yourself in someone.

In those moments, you are no longer two separate people. You are life, speaking with itself, experiencing its reason for being.

Impermanence is the idea that
everything changes, forever.

We hold on to what's familiar because we think it will make us feel safe, but often it just makes life feel smaller and repetitive.

If we look deeply at impermanence, we see that change isn't only about what we lose. It's also about what's constantly coming into existence.

When we see this, we stop fearing change so much. We stop clinging to the familiar and start living with curiosity, openness, and a sense that life is always unfolding into something beautifully new.

Holding on to resentment seems like
a useful way to punish someone you're
upset with. The truth is that they don't feel it.
They go on with their lives, not thinking of
you at all, while your resentment
harms someone else.

You.

Letting go of those heavy emotions keeps
you from living in unnecessary pain and
passing that pain on to others.

Stand up for yourself and expect respect.
But don't hold on to embers of anger
when you're the one being burned.

Living impulsively can be exciting. It brings
novelty, stimulation, and a sense of aliveness.

But balance is key. Without intention,
that wild energy turns into chaos.

Intentional choices give your life direction.
They turn scattered moments into a path,
one that is fulfilling instead of fleeting.

We are sold the story that to feel truly alive, we must chase great peaks and exotic experiences. The truth is that those extremes move us only because the experiences themselves awaken a mindset that reveals the sheer brilliance of human existence.

You don't need an extraordinary experience to see the magnificence of being alive. The great mystery lives in the most ordinary experiences. The real art is to kindle that mindset from within, rather than waiting for circumstances to do it for you.

Look deeply at the present moment. Consider the impossible magic that you are a conscious being who is aware of your own awareness, experiencing the timeless moment of now, while floating in the infinite expanse of the universe. Feel the gravity of being alive, and know that if you peer into the present with deep attention, in its truest nature, you will forever find profound insight woven into ordinary experiences.

Every moment of awareness

is a moment of enlightenment.

04 BECOME

Be the person who radiates calm.
Heal your mind, let go of attachments
that trigger tension, trust how you feel,
know your worth, and release into this
moment. Move through life knowing
that this is all temporary, so you're going
to lead with love, compassion, and clarity.
Then watch how your energy helps
other people feel that way too.

Do less. But do it deeply.

Scattering your attention scatters
your purpose, and that scatters
your happiness.

If something isn't worth spending
much time on, it might not be worth
spending *any* time on.

UNDERRATED LIFE SKILL:

Knowing when to let your

silence say everything.

You don't have to escape

your life to feel peaceful.

You have to shift how you

relate to what's already there.

Bring your quiet, slow, patient,

mindful, sturdy self into how you:

Wake, work, walk, talk, listen, and love.

Then you're no longer chasing the idea

that you can make your *life* peaceful.

You're learning instead to make

yourself peaceful within your life.

The more clearly you

see yourself, the less reactive

you are to how others see you.

Emotions will always expand and contract.

That's the rhythm of being human.

The sooner we accept that tension is part of life, the sooner we can learn to release it.

When tension arises, don't push it down.

Notice it. Label the sensation.

Naming your emotion creates space.

From that space, you can see what sparked the tension more clearly and respond with compassion.

Life will never be free of emotional tension.

But we can learn to process it, with smooth wisdom, instead of clinging to it and letting it control us.

Letting go becomes a natural reflex. It takes effort at first, but with practice, you'll start responding with pause, insight, and precision rather than agitation.

The skill starts small and fades in, getting a little stronger each day. One day, you find yourself in a situation where you'd normally react, close off, or attack, and you notice spaciousness in your thoughts.

In that space, you slow down, mindfully navigate the moment, and act with intention, instead of reactivity. Then it hits you that your mindful awareness has grown.

Move through your day with softness.

Walk a little slower and breathe a little deeper.

Embrace gentleness as a way of being, and treat
each moment, word, look, and touch with the
tenderness it truly deserves.

All things in life are impermanent, here
in one second and gone the next.

When you are with them in the present,
you share a moment of infinity.

As you take the quiet with you,
you'll notice that you start seeing
ordinary things differently.

The small, gentle, and fleeting will
feel meaningful. The big, flashy,
and loud will become uninteresting.

You'll feel the calm vibrating in the
present moment. You'll survey reality
from a distance and up close at once.

Every time your eyes meet another's,
you'll generate peaceful warmth. And
heart energy will flow through you.

SLOW EXPERIMENT:

Do one thing 50 percent slower than usual today. Notice what you observe. Notice how it feels to move at your own pace instead of the world's.

It's not just about learning
how to be calm in stressful
moments.

It's about living a calm life
so that when stress arrives,
it's nothing more than a
small drop in an ocean of
understanding.

A clear sign of growth is when
you can be around tense people
without becoming one yourself.

Grounding yourself through wisdom,
self-observation, and emotional clarity
creates a strong physical presence.

To the outside world, it looks as though
you are impenetrable, as though anger,
tension, and fear flow around you.

In truth, you are open, always
receiving without grasping.

It's not that you shield yourself from the
noise of the world. It's that you let it
pass through you.

You can tell when someone is full
of wisdom and presence. As your eyes
catch theirs, you spot a knowing twinkle,
like light bouncing off glass, that lets you
know they can see the magic in life too.

SIGNS OF WISDOM:

Quick to laugh

Smiles generously

Always learning more

Takes nothing personally

Radiates warmth and calm

Accepts others without judging

Sees everything with a curious eye

Listens to understand, not just respond

Peace grows from the inside out.

The path may seem long, but it becomes
much shorter when you break it into pieces.

Growth isn't about making big changes
all at once.

It's doing your best in each moment to see
yourself clearly without holding yourself
to unrealistic perfection.

Over time, those small daily efforts of clarity,
compassion, and calm will reshape your mind.

Patience and consistency are rewarded a little
more each day. Lightness slowly swells, and
you feel at home, wherever you may be.

Your days are made up of
small moments. Treat each one
as special, gentle, and sacred, and
your whole life will feel so.

Every moment offers a choice to react or respond, to be numb or present, to judge or lovingly observe, to listen to the noise or listen within, to be possessed by your pain or heal it.

Choose the path that brings you home to a feeling of harmony, a sensation of levitation, a calm trust in your integrity, and a known sense of alignment.

Make this mindful choice, again and again, and the tone of your life will hum with peace.

Think back to how noisy your mind was,
how much tension you held in your body,
and how little control you had over yourself.

Look at where you are today. More clarity
and intention. You did that. You saw how you
wanted to change and put in the effort
to give yourself a better life.

Imagine what could happen if you keep going.

Consider that the same amount of growth you've
noticed between your past and your present is possible
between your present and your future.

That life is waiting for you.

Keep choosing what feels right.

Keep looking deeply.

Keep listening within.

UNDERRATED LIFE SKILL:

Moving calmly in a world

addicted to reactions.

Slow living is not a single thing.

It is the way you do everything,

with presence instead of hurry.

Every message doesn't need an instant reply.

Every moment doesn't need to be productive.

Every hobby doesn't have to be monetized.

Every little chat doesn't need a strategy.

When you stop trying to optimize your life,

you find that simply living in the flow of the

present makes *everything* optimal.

The moment you stop needing people
to understand your path is the moment
you start walking it freely.

Peace is not *where* you are.
It's *how* you engage with
what's before you. Take the
quiet with you, and you will
find calm in every step.

Quiet brings slowness.

Slowness brings clarity.

Clarity brings insight.

Insight brings perspective.

Perspective brings wisdom.

Wisdom brings peace.

There is great freedom

in knowing you are allowed

to be unreachable.

Don't fear calm.

Don't fear quiet.

Don't fear stillness.

They aren't cold.

They aren't dark.

They aren't empty.

They invite you to see.

They invite you to hear.

They invite you to feel.

Clarity of mind.

Clarity of heart.

Clarity of truth.

When the mind is quiet,

even a single drop of rain

becomes a revelation.

Perspective is everything. Look at the world as a cold machine or a magical mystery, and whichever one you believe, you'll be right.

Not because the universe is either of those things. But because what you look for is what you'll see.

If you look for anger and pain, you'll find them. If you look for beauty and love, you'll find them too.

Consciousness is highly shapeable. Since we aren't taught this, our minds run wild, focusing on what reinforces our current emotions and biases.

However, we can develop conscious focus. Pay attention to the goodness in the world. Spend time with wholesome people. Look for potentials instead of faults. Choose optimism. Seek light.

This is how you take charge of your reality. Focus on what's good in you and in the world. You won't only start to see more magic. You'll feel it too.

When your mind is quiet, it is clear.

Clarity gives you more perspective.

Perspective shows you many paths.

One path will always be harmony.

The real flex is refusing

to let a harsh world

make you harsh too.

SIMPLE JOYS:

Taking a breath of fresh air.

Feeling sunlight on your skin.

Hearing leaves dance in the trees.

Releasing the muscles in your body.

Letting yourself be held by the universe.

Watching calm clouds move across the sky.

Feeling your feet touch the earth as you walk.

Becoming peaceful isn't about how
much you can relax your body.

Peace is an intention.

With every thought, act, and response,
you are choosing balance and harmony.

The universe is chaotic. Tension will find you.
Some seasons will be heavy. Some will be hard.

Don't expect yourself to be perfectly serene.
Just remember that whether life feels smooth
or sharp, you can still choose peace.

Choose to calm, not inflame. Set your ego aside
and work from your heart. See through the noise
and into enlightenment.

Every time you pause to breathe
before you act, you're choosing to
lead with clarity instead of chaos.

HOW TO FEEL FREE:

Rest without guilt.

Let go of old anger.

Respect your worth.

Spend time in silence.

Move at your own pace.

Speak kindly to yourself.

Forgive your previous self.

Making assumptions about other people's thoughts, actions, or motives writes a story in your mind that feels real and creates genuine tension.

The mind constantly fills in gaps, trying to protect you by preparing you for what might happen.

But these assumptions usually come from emotional states like anxiety, frustration, or insecurity, which means they are built on fear rather than truth.

When you recognize these mental stories, you create space between what is actually happening in reality and what your mind is imagining.

In that space, the story falls apart and you see clearly again. You can then carry on and meet life as it is, instead of your idea of what it is going to be.

Clear communication without
judgment, assumption, or imposed
emotion is the most direct path
to authentic connection.

Mental clarity isn't having a mind
without thoughts.

It is recognizing your thoughts for
what they are—temporary mental
formations—and choosing to use
them mindfully or let them go.

There is so much peace in treating
the mental chatter of your ego like the
aimless background noise that it is.

Being present makes the days longer
when the years keep feeling shorter.

In this time, be with who you love.
Let meaningless tension fall away.
Know the true meaning of life.
Surrender to compassion.

A BEAUTIFUL LOVE:

When you feel the most at peace

simply being in the present together.

The mind speeds up when stimulation increases because it's trying to keep pace with its environment.

Spending time in quiet, calm stillness is a valuable training ground. It gives you time to decompress, let your guard down, and develop self-intimacy.

This builds a sturdy, mindful awareness that you can take with you in life. You can then return to that calm energy when you find yourself in stimulating situations.

Consistently spending time in stillness increases your capacity for calm mental clarity. Eventually, you need quiet space less, because the stillness is no longer outside of you. It's within you.

Once you start watching your mind, it becomes
quite funny. So many angles of perception, stories
spinning up, strategies, protection mechanisms,
and reasons to validate craving.

Looking deeply at the chatter of your mind and
understanding it for the kaleidoscope of noise
that it is takes the seriousness out of everything.

It helps you see the real you, the observer behind
the thoughts, who is peacefully experiencing
the conscious texture of it all.

Here, you can pause, let the thoughts
flow around you like the wind, and patiently
choose the guidance of reflective wisdom.

May you feel more nostalgia for the present.

Just as others reflect on the comforting warmth
of the past, may you reflect on the brilliant,
precious now.

May you feel that this moment is already
the perfect memory.

Many times a day, may you be moved, struck,
and awed as your heart pours open with gratitude
for simply being here, immersed in
the wonder of it all.

Calm is a wisdom that turns

patience into power.

A quiet mind sees agitation,
impulse, and reaction as they
appear and lets them go.

A quiet mind sees anxiety,
shyness, and uncertainty
and offers loving support.

A quiet mind sees laughter,
warmth, and joy and takes
the time to soak them in.

A quiet mind sees the stress,
worry, and fear that life brings
and gracefully releases them.

Urgency is a habit, not a truth.

When you slow down, you realize
that most things are not as immediate
as they once seemed.

The illusion everyone else is chasing
becomes clear.

You feel compassion for those around
you and free from the pressure to
live like a machine.

Slow down.

Not to fall behind.

But to finally arrive.

05 ARISE

It's wild that when you decide
you're worth more, the universe starts
opening doors to make it a reality.

REMEMBER:

People's opinions of you are
more about them than you.

Sometimes growth is asking
other people to relearn you.

You're not cold for setting
boundaries. You're clear.

You have a life to live,
not a story to defend.

Once the mind is calm,
the body calms too.

Peace is seen in your physical
expression. Movements become slower
and more fluid and intentional.

Your presence reflects inner calm,
and you signal perceptual clarity,
warmth, and wisdom to
those around you.

Those signals make the people in
your life feel at ease, open, and safe.

When you order your inner world,
you also order the world around you.

Keep putting your good energy
into the world. It's helping people
around you more than you know.

Waking your mind up from autopilot brings you into the present. As you watch your mind, you work in real time with your inner life. You see how arising thoughts, emotions, and impulses fluidly feed into what you're experiencing in each moment.

Clarity at this level gives you awareness of the subtle movements inside and outside of you. This lets you move your ego aside and engage with life mindfully. You monitor yourself in the present, notice negative reactions arising in you, and let them go. You guide each word toward egoless love.

Read this closely. Read it again when needed. It is a description and reminder of the work that will create the peaceful life you've been searching for.

Making the most of life
isn't about doing more. It's
about being more aligned.

When we want others to change, we just want them to become more like us.

Let go of judging people based on how they meet your personal preferences. It opens up a whole new dimension of life.

Meet people where they are. It lets you actually meet *them,* rather than just your idea of them.

Original Mind is awareness before preference, judgment, and the past telling you what the present means. It's the part of you that sees reality clearly, free from personal bias.

When you approach life with this kind of mind—less attached, less certain, and more curious—you begin to feel a new sense of wonder. You're so present that everything feels new, like you're a tourist in your hometown.

You stop fighting life as it is and understand that freedom comes from living without the past constantly interpreting the present.

UNDERRATED LIFE SKILL:

Not taking your thoughts personally.

SIGNS OF WISDOM:

Seeks growth in subtle, everyday ways.

Pauses to separate reaction from reality.

Uses words to inspire rather than criticize.

Sees possibilities where others see obstacles.

Communicates clearly, even when it's hard.

Takes responsibility for choices and actions.

Releases mental stories before they take over.

Allows growth to unfold instead of forcing it.

Builds calm by taking deep, intentional breaths.

Remains open to being wrong and learning more.

Speaks with awareness of how words affect others.

Considers multiple perspectives before concluding.

Holds emotions without taking them out on others.

When you stop worrying

about being no one, you

start to become someone.

There is no peace if you can't be who you are.

You can't be who you are without looking within.

You can't look within if you can't clear your mind.

You can't clear your mind without sitting in quiet.

Remember these
five guides when
you feel lost:

Pause

Breath

Silence

Patience

Presence

They will always
be there when
you need them.

Be the person who sees clearly.
React less to the world around
you, calmly observe reality, relax
your body, communicate with
care, ignore mental stories, and
always listen to what feels right.

Courage isn't loud.

It's a quiet clarity that

says, "Not this anymore."

Building a better life is thought of as adding
new habits to your routine. But that's
only half of the process.

The other half is removing.

Look honestly at the habits and people
that are with you.

Listen closely to your gut. Honor its signal when
it tells you what no longer belongs in your life.

Let go and clear away.

Make room for what's trying to arrive.

Going from being worried about
what might happen to being excited
about what might happen is only
a mindset shift away.

The mind tries to talk us out of change because the familiar feels safe, even if it's holding us back. It will use anxiety, projections, and self-limiting thoughts to delay us.

Remember that the mind is as flexible as it is powerful. It runs different sets of thoughts—like apps running in the background—and it defaults to the ones you've used the most. This is why shifting those mental patterns is called a mindset shift.

As the mind tries to talk you out of change, switch the set it's running. Choose thoughts rooted in abundance rather than fear. Imagine the potential for incredible things to happen instead of rehearsing the worst. Watch how that shift changes the energy in your body and the flow of your mind.

Stop delaying the start to

the best years of your life.

GENTLE REMINDER:

You might not need more advice.
You might just need to finally do
what you know you need to.

MINDSET:

Trust how your path is unfolding
while choosing what feels right
again and again.

A good life is thinking, *Every day, I'm going to let go of the habits that weigh me down and create habits that lift me up.*

Things won't change overnight, and you wouldn't want them to. If life could transform for the better in an instant, it could just as easily turn the other way.

Inner change is a gradual process of awareness, discovery, and refinement.

First, your awareness expands, and you begin observing your patterns, thoughts, and reactions.

As you feel your intuition telling you that something is out of alignment, you discover a growth area.

Then, you nurture your evolution by refining that pattern, thought, or reaction.

Following this process chips away at your unconscious habits. You grow a little each day, forever guiding yourself toward more wisdom, clarity, and well-being.

Keep believing.

The mind will go through periods
of self-doubt and fear of the future.

These are the moments when you
must find your grit and move forward
into the unknown, rather than stay
still and suffer in the storm.

REMINDERS WHILE ON THE PATH:

Love others, but don't sacrifice your self-love.

Question thoughts, but listen to your intuition.

Explore new things, but stay true to your path.

Remain focused, but don't use focus to escape.

Help others, but don't do the work for them.

Respect yourself, but always stay humble.

The real flex is not needing to flex
at all because you stopped basing your
worth on the opinions of others.

Inner peace isn't just useful because
it feels good to be calm. It's a method
of grounding that evolves into self-trust.

This resilience prepares you for unknown
territory, arming you with sturdy mindfulness,
clear vision, and emotional clarity.

Putting in the work to keep your
mind clear and your body calm is
the best investment you can make
in your future.

Self-discipline is self-love.

Choosing to prioritize good health,
kind people, and a clear mindset
over quick pleasure shows that you
care about yourself in the present
and have faith that big things are
coming to you in the future.

When you're working to evolve,
you're affirming to yourself that
you trust a better life is coming.

The world is loud and always seeking
your attention. It will try to pull you
into its urgency, outrage, and
endless distractions.

Clarity and inner peace protect you
from being drawn into life's drama.
They help you see the noise without
becoming the noise, step back without
disconnecting, and continue living
with your mental freedom.

Your environment shapes your mind
more than you might think.

Design your space so distractions are
out of sight and supportive tools
are easy to access.

Put meaningful books where you'll
see them. Keep your phone out of reach.
Make your meditation cushion visible.
Always have a glass of water nearby.

When your living space is set up well,
good habits become easier to follow.

You create less resistance to growth
and stay aligned with the life
you want to live.

Quiet calms the nervous system.

Resentment clouds the mind.

Stillness reveals direction.

Envy drains energy.

Gratitude gives life.

Breathing grounds.

Being happy all the time isn't the goal. That's not how life works. The goal is to make the heavy parts of your life lighter so that although you may not be happy every day, your years will always be rooted in joy.

You feel an energy building when you start to see change in your life. As you continue to release past emotional pain, something in your body and mind lets go. The lightness feels so liberating. It almost feels like you're floating.

Witnessing your work pay off, from the inside out, creates an inner momentum that shows you just how much potential your life holds.

Yet everything in the universe expands and contracts. While you're riding your newfound flow of energy, don't be discouraged when you hit a lull. It will happen.

When it does, remember that life force comes in waves. They rise, and they will fall. The key is not forgetting, when the waves fall, that they will always rise again and take you even closer to the other shore.

Ride the energy that flows
from the quiet, but don't mistake
your ego for *its* power.

Once the garden of the mind is weeded of thought fragments, distractions, and emotional tension, the mental energy you once used to manage that chaos becomes available.

That's why when the mind is quiet and the body is calm, powerful energy begins to surge through your consciousness.

Use this energy wisely.

Direct it toward positive goals. Focus it on a clean inner vision. Manage it well, and let it flow into everything you encounter, and it will elevate the landscape of your entire life.

MINDSET:

Slow down, be present,

feel the depth of being alive,

and don't forget that it's

love over everything.

If you slow down enough,
you can get to a place where
you have no preferences.

It's not that you don't like
anything or don't care.

It's that you're so present
you can see the brilliance
and joy in everything.

Perception is the key to freedom.

(Sit with this)

When you *know* that we are all
experiencing different versions
of reality, you are free.

(Sit with this)

Compassion, curiosity, patience,
presence, and understanding
become all that is useful.

(Sit with this)

Seeing that even *your* reality
is a mental story helps you stop
taking life so personally and start
focusing on loving clarity.

(Sit with this)

When you catch yourself looking down
on someone, remember that you were
once standing where they are.

At some point in your life, someone said
something that shifted your perspective.
It opened your mind, and suddenly, you
could see more clearly. You realized there
was more to learn, more to understand,
and more ways to grow.

Instead of judging others for not seeing
what you see, try to be the person who
gently turns on the light, just as
someone once did for you.

You'll know you have gained wisdom
once you notice that your perception has
fooled you again (and again and again).

REMEMBER:

Wisdom doesn't only live in the mind.

It speaks through emotions too.

But in symbols, not words.

From body, not brain.

You become a powerful force when you quiet your inner life so that you can see your mind clearly, hear the wisdom in your emotions, follow your intuition, and let life unfold instead of forcing it.

Nurture these qualities and weave them together so they become fluid and flexible as they interact with the world.

Grasp at nothing and receive everything.

Through effortless action, you can move through life with a presence that radiates calm, feels timeless, fosters instant trust, and shines as a beacon of insight.

Flowing with this essence of liberation reveals an enlightened life, not only for you, but for all those who surround you.

(This points to the way)

Arise beyond the patterns that kept you stuck.

Arise beyond the reactions that controlled you.

Arise beyond the thoughts that clouded your mind.

Arise beyond the emotions that weighed on you.

Arise beyond the stories that insisted you couldn’t.

Arise beyond the belief that you were never enough.

Arise.

Arise into a life of mental clarity and understanding.

Arise into a life of emotional wisdom and feeling.

Arise into a life of nervous system regulation.

Arise into a life of self-respect and self-love.

Arise into a life of limitless possibilities.

Arise into a life of spiritual freedom.

Arise.

MINDSET:

Trusting that
the most beautiful
moments of your life
are still to come.

your

quiet

age

has

begun

ABOUT THE AUTHOR

CORY ALLEN is a writer, speaker, mindfulness expert, and podcaster. His work focuses on helping people slow down, think clearly, and reconnect with themselves in a fast, overstimulated world. His writing on Instagram reaches millions each week, offering simple, grounded insights for those seeking more calm, clarity, and intention. With over twenty-five years of experience in mindfulness, meditation, and self-inquiry, Cory distills complex inner work into practical, embodied wisdom.

The authorised representative in the EEA is Simon and Schuster Netherlands BV, Herculesplein 96 3584 AA Utrecht, Netherlands. (info@simonandschuster.nl)

Andrews McMeel Publishing
a division of Andrews McMeel Universal
1130 Walnut Street, Kansas City, Missouri 64106

www.andrewsmcmeel.com

26 27 28 29 30 VEP 10 9 8 7 6 5 4 3 2 1

ISBN: 979-8-8816-0984-9

Library of Congress Control Number: 2026943771

FSC www.fsc.org MIX Paper | Supporting responsible forestry FSC® C005010

ATTENTION: SCHOOLS AND BUSINESSES
Andrews McMeel books are available at quantity discounts with bulk purchase for educational, business, or sales promotional use. For information, please email the Andrews McMeel Publishing Special Sales Department: sales@andrewsmcmeel.com.